# The MAILBOX

The Education Center

# Pond

M000274287

THE BEST OF
The MAILBOX
MAGAZINE

**Our best pond activities and reproducibles from the 1998–2007 issues of** *The Mailbox* **and** *Teacher's Helper* **magazines**

- **Literacy activities**
- **Learning centers**
- **Group-time activities**
- **Songs, poems, and fingerplays**

- **Math activities**
- **Arts-and-crafts ideas**
- **...and more!**

*Fun and practical skills practice!*

**Managing Editor:** Tina Petersen

**Editorial Team:** Becky S. Andrews, Diane Badden, Kimberley Bruck, Karen A. Brudnak, Pam Crane, Tazmen Hansen, Marsha Heim, Lori Z. Henry, Debra Liverman, Kitty Lowrance, Jennifer Nunn, Mark Rainey, Hope Rodgers, Rebecca Saunders, Rachael Traylor, Sharon M. Tresino, Zane Williard

# www.themailbox.com

©2010 The Mailbox® Books
All rights reserved.
ISBN10 #1-56234-915-5 • ISBN13 #978-1-56234-915-8

# Table of Contents

## Thematic Units

# Fantastic FROG centers!

Dive into this collection of frog-themed centers and watch your little tadpoles jump for joy!

*ideas contributed by Lucia Kemp Henry*
*Fallon, NV*

## Science Center
### That's Life!

*Exploring the life cycle of a frog*

Eggs, tadpoles, and frogs—oh, my! This science center reinforces the different stages of a frog's life. Make two copies of the frog life cycle patterns on page 7. Color the patterns, laminate them for durability, and cut them out. Then ready the cutouts for flannelboard use. Also, cut from felt the following shapes: a large blue pond, a brown log, and green lily pads. Place the prepared props near your flannelboard. Before introducing the center, acquaint youngsters with the life cycle of a frog through a read-aloud book, such as *Frogs* by Gail Gibbons. Then invite youngsters to the center to tell the story of a frog's life!

## Sensory Center
### Fancy Frogs

*Developing the sense of touch, sorting by pattern*

Stripes, dots, and zigzags! The fancy frogs in this tub are perfect for sorting! Fill a plastic tub with assorted lengths of blue crepe paper (for water). Next, make a template of the swimming frog pattern on page 8. Trace the template onto green craft foam to make six or more frogs. Use three different designs to decorate the frogs, repeating each design as often as desired. Then cut out the frog shapes and scatter them under the crepe paper water. A student removes the frogs from the water and sorts them by their designs!

### Fine-Motor Center
## EGGS Aplenty!
*Developing fine-motor skills*

The results of this fine-motor practice make an "egg-stra" special addition to a pond display! Provide randomly cut pieces of bubble wrap and two or three black fine-tip permanent markers at a table. Little ones transform the bubble wrap pieces into frog eggs by carefully drawing a black dot in the center of each bubble! Plan to display the eggs at a pond display like the one shown on page 35.

Nancy M. Lotzer
Farmers Branch, TX

### Puzzle Center
## Lily Pad Puzzlers
*Developing spatial awareness*

When each of these lily pad puzzles is put together, a lucky little frog has a perfect place to perch! Make five colorful construction paper copies of the large frog pattern on page 7 and draw an equal number of lily pads on green construction paper. Laminate the patterns and cut them out. Then cut each lily pad into two pieces, using a different puzzle cut each time. Place the cutouts at a center. A youngster completes each lily pad puzzle and tops it off with a frog cutout. Ribbit!

bee

### Literacy Center
## Frogs and Logs
*Identifying rhymes*

What better way to practice rhyme identification than by setting frogs on logs? Make eight green construction paper copies of the large frog pattern on page 7 and one copy of the rhyming cards on page 8. Color the cards, cut them out, and then sort them into four sets of three rhyming cards each. Glue one card from each set onto a 3" x 12" strip of brown construction paper. Glue each remaining card onto a different frog. Laminate the pieces for durability, cut out each frog, and trim each brown paper strip into a log shape. A youngster chooses a frog and names its picture. Then he sets the frog on the log that has a rhyming picture. He continues until each frog is sitting on a log.

## Flannelboard Center
# A Speckled Sing-Along
*Counting, showing understanding of a song*

Pair the popular preschool song "Five Green and Speckled Frogs" with counting practice, and math skills will grow by leaps and bounds! Cut from brown felt a log shape that is approximately 8 inches long. Next, reduce the large frog pattern on page 7 to 50 percent; then make five green construction paper copies of the reduced frog pattern. Use markers to add speckles to the log and to each frog. Laminate the frogs for durability, cut them out, and ready each one for flannelboard use. Practice the song "Five Green and Speckled Frogs" with students. (Or provide a recording of the song at the center.) A student places the felt log on the flannelboard and then she sets the five frogs atop the log. As she sings the song, she removes the frogs from the log. For added fun, tape a blue poster board pocket to the bottom of the flannelboard. (See the illustration.) When it's time for a frog to jump off a log, a youngster drops it inside the pocket! Glub, glub!

Lenny D. Grozier
Binghamton, NY

## Art Center
# Spots on Frogs!
*Exploring texture*

Painting spots on frogs? Why not? To make a spot stamper, cut a one-inch shape and a two-inch shape from a textured material such as corrugated cardboard, bubble wrap, or mesh shelf liner. Hot-glue the cutouts to opposite ends of an empty film canister. Make as many stampers as desired. Store the stampers (small shapes up) in an empty tray. Place the tray, shallow containers of tempera paint, and a class supply of large frog cutouts at a center. (If desired, enlarge the large frog pattern from page 7.) Each preschooler paints an assortment of spots on his frog, feeling each texture as he paints with it. Hey, these spotted frogs are spiffy!

Amy Shimelman—PreK
JCAA Early Childhood Program
Austin, TX

## Water Table
# Splish, Splash!
*Exploration through pretend play*

Floating lily pads and plastic frogs make the water table a "ribbiting" destination! Trim two or more kitchen sponges into lily pad shapes. Then put the sponge cutouts and a few plastic frogs at your water table. Invite little ones to use the supplies to explore a variety of froggy behaviors, such as sitting on a lily pad, hopping into the water, and swimming! Whew!

Lenny D. Grozier
Binghamton, NY

*jennifer tipton bennett*

## Math Center
# Feast for Froggy
*Counting, recognizing numerals*

Watch little ones gather lickety-split to this center to feed pom-pom bugs to a froggy! Copy the large frog pattern from page 7 onto green construction paper and cut five 1½" x 6" strips of pink construction paper for tongues. Label the bottom of each tongue with a different number from 1 to 5. Then laminate and cut out the frog pattern and strips. To the front of each tongue, attach Velcro dots (hook side) to match the programmed number. Also attach the hook side of a Velcro dot just below the frog's mouth. Then, to the back of each tongue, near the top, attach the loop side of a Velcro dot. Place the prepared pieces at a center along with 15 pom-poms for bugs. A youngster attaches a tongue to the frog. She counts orally as she puts a bug on each Velcro dot. Then she removes the tongue. She repeats the procedure with each tongue. Wow! That frog caught three bugs at one time!

## Reading Area
# "Pond-ering" Good Books
*Demonstrating an interest in independent reading*

Motivate youngsters to investigate frog-themed books at this peaceful classroom pond! Place a blue blanket on the floor to represent water and add a few green pillows for lily pads. Provide a supply of frog-themed books. For added ambiance, softly play a recording of rushing water or frog sounds. If desired, also enlist your youngsters' help in making cattails from construction paper and gift wrap tubes. (See the illustration.) Display the cattails around the pond in weighted containers. Little ones are sure to enjoy this "un-frog-getable" reading area!

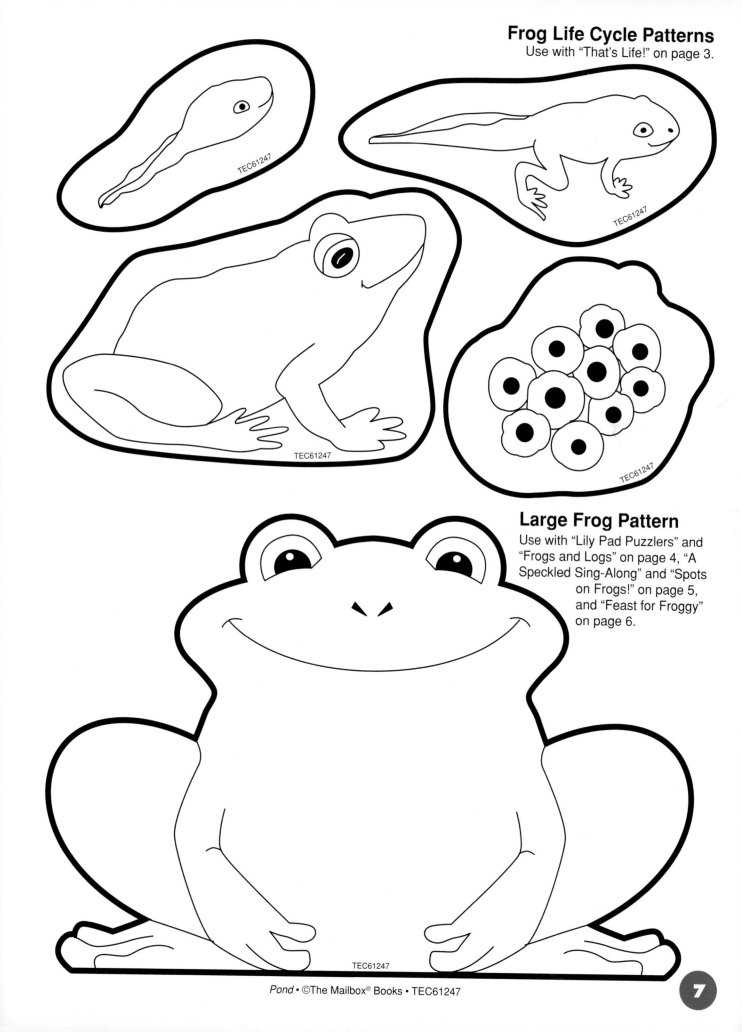

## Frog Life Cycle Patterns
Use with "That's Life!" on page 3.

TEC61247

TEC61247

TEC61247

TEC61247

## Large Frog Pattern
Use with "Lily Pad Puzzlers" and "Frogs and Logs" on page 4, "A Speckled Sing-Along" and "Spots on Frogs!" on page 5, and "Feast for Froggy" on page 6.

TEC61247

# Swimming Frog Pattern
Use with "Fancy Frogs" on page 3.

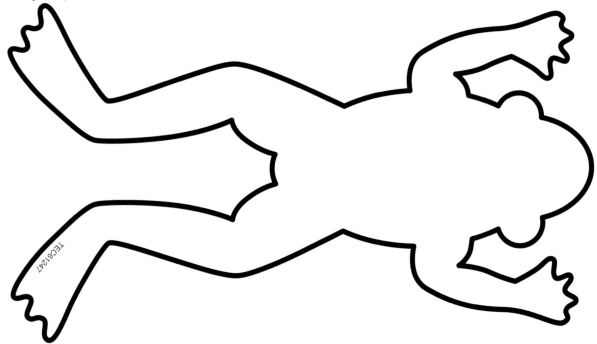

# Rhyming Cards
Use with "Frogs and Logs" on page 4.

*Pond* • ©The Mailbox® Books • TEC61247

# Frog Follies

Jeepers creepers, take a look at these leapers! Turn your preschoolers into hopped-up herpetologists by introducing them to some fun facts about frogs: how they grow up, where they live, what they eat, and how they get around. You're never too young to leap into learning!

ideas contributed by Henry Fergus—Preschool,
Desert View Elementary, Phoenix, AZ

## An Awesome Amphibian

### *Motivation*

"Ribbit" youngsters' attention to your frog theme with this friendly fellow. To make a beanbag frog, cut out two same-sized, five-inch-long ovals from green felt. Also cut out two webbed feet. Sandwich the feet and a two-inch length of red ribbon between the ovals as shown; then hot-glue the ovals together, leaving an opening. Fill the shape with beans; then hot-glue the opening closed. Finally, hot-glue on two white pom-poms and two paper eyes to complete the frog.

Use this frog to introduce a different froggy fact each day. In addition, seat him on your shoulder while reading frog-related stories or use him as a positive-behavior motivator by seating him on a child's shoulder. Also use him for the hopping game described in "Come On Over to My Pad" on page 10. Ribbit!

### Froggy Facts

**Frogs grow and change.**
Tadpoles are frog babies. A tadpole has a tail and swims in the water. It grows back legs and then front legs. Next, it climbs out of the water. Its tail gets smaller until it disappears. The tadpole has grown into a frog!

### *Fish Is Fish*
Written & Illustrated by Leo Lionni

## Frog Song

### *Investigating living things*

Kids grow and change, and frogs do too! Simplify the text of an informative book such as Gail Gibbons's *Frogs* to introduce your little ones to a frog's growing pattern. Then invite them to sing the following song.

### Frogs Grow and Change
*(sung to the tune of "The Frog Went A-courtin' ")*

Did you know frogs grow and change? Uh-huh, uh-huh.
Did you know frogs grow and change? Uh-huh, uh-huh.
[A tadpole is a baby frog. It moves its tail to swim along.]
Now we know frogs grow and change. Uh-huh. Uh-huh.

### Continue with the following:
*Its back legs are the first to grow; then its front legs start to show.*
*It climbs onto the land that's near; now its tail can disappear.*
*The frog's back legs grow big and strong; it uses them to hop along.*

## Froggy Facts

**Frogs jump and swim.** Frogs have long, strong back legs that make them good jumpers. Their webbed toes help them swim fast.

*Hop Jump*
Written & Illustrated by Ellen Stoll Walsh

## Come On Over to My Pad

Prepare at least a class supply of laminated, green construction-paper lily pads. Then use them over and over as you leap from one of the following activities to the next.

• Arrange the lily pads in your group area to indicate seating spaces.

• Label one side of each pad with a colorful shape; then use the pads as a transition tool. For example, announce, "Everyone seated on a lily pad with a square, line up" or "Everyone seated on a lily pad with a yellow shape, pick a center."

• Arrange a number of lily pads in a path to make a giant gameboard. To play a counting game, invite several children to pretend to be frogs. On each child's turn, roll a large die. Have the child count the dots and then hop down the path that number of lily pads. Every child is a winner when he arrives at the end of the path and jumps onto the land.

• Use the lily pads to play a variation of Musical Chairs. As lily pads are removed, encourage your little frogs to share the remaining pads so that no frogs end up in the pond.

• Label one side of each pad with a numeral. Arrange the pads, numeral sides up, in an open area. Give a volunteer from the group the bean-bag frog described in "An Awesome Amphibian" (page 9). Have the child toss the frog onto a pad and then announce that pad's numeral. Invite the children to hop that number of times.

## Pond, Sweet Pond

### Art

"Pond-ering" how to teach youngsters about a frog's habitat? Here's a craft they'll jump at the chance to make. To make one, paint a rock green. When the paint is dry, glue on paper eyes. Next, glue pieces of grass and twigs onto a white, sterilized Styrofoam tray. When the glue is dry, cover the tray with blue plastic wrap, securing the wrap to the back of the tray with tape. Finally, glue the rock frog onto a construction-paper lily pad. Place the frog on top of the pond. Display each child's pond on a low surface along with his dictation of something he has learned about frogs or something he likes about frogs.

Frogs hop really great!
Christopher

## Pond Companions

### Animal habitats

Take a frog's-eye peek at pond life by reading aloud *In the Small, Small Pond* by Denise Fleming. Ask students to name as many animals as they can remember that share a frog's home. Then prepare this group-time graphing activity to plunge into over and over again. In advance, cut out ten each of yellow duck shapes, orange fish shapes, and green frog shapes. Also prepare a 3 square x 10 square graph on a length of bulletin-board paper. To begin, scatter several lily pads (see "Come On Over to My Pad" on page 10) and a number of the cutouts onto an open area. Ask how many of each animal are living in the pond. Collect, count, and then graph the cutouts. Each round, develop math skills by asking questions such as "Are there more frogs or ducks in this pond?" or "Is there a fish friend for every frog in our pond?" Now that's an activity that'll keep 'em pondering!

## Frog Frolic

### Tossing

Transform your water table into a pond for your little ones' exploration. Simply tint the water blue and add aquarium plants and craft-foam lily-pad cutouts. If desired, spray-paint a number of Ping-Pong balls green; then use a permanent marker to add facial features to each one. Encourage a child to stand away from the water-table pond and then try to toss a frog onto a floating pad.

# Duck Detail

Waddle into spring with this duck unit, which focuses on all areas of the curriculum.

ideas by Angie Kutzer, Garrett Elementary, Mebane, NC

### Ducks on the Pond
*Rhyming*

Youngsters splash around with rhyming words in this pocket chart pond. Cut out 20 construction paper duck shapes (or use pages from a small duck-shaped notepad). Copy the rhyming pictures on page 15 and then cut them apart. Glue a picture to the back of each duck and then insert the ducks picture-side down into a pocket chart. Have each child, in turn, choose two ducks and then name the pictures on each one. If the words rhyme, encourage the rest of the class to give two energetic quacks; then instruct the child to place the cutouts picture-side up in the chart. If the pictures do not rhyme, have students give one sad quack. Instruct the child to return the ducks picture-side down in their original positions. Continue in this manner until all ducks have been paired. Then place the pocket chart and cutouts in your literacy center to encourage more rhyme-matching fun!

### A Duck's Favorite Sound
*Identifying same beginning sounds*

This idea helps youngsters learn to listen for beginning sounds in words. Glue a blue pond cutout onto white bulletin board paper. Glue a duck cutout to the center of the pond. Cut a supply of pictures from old magazines, most of which begin with the letter *d* and a few that do not. During circle time, place the prepared paper in the center of the circle and give each child a picture. Have each student, in turn, decide whether her picture begins with the /d/ sound. Instruct her to glue the picture on the pond if it begins with /d/ or glue it on the area around the pond if it does not start with /d/. Continue until each child has added her pictures to the chart; then review the *d* pictures in the pond. Just ducky!

## Singing Sounds
### Identifying sounds

Put the knowledge of the sound of the letter *d* to music with this quick and catchy tune. Write the verse on sentence strips and place them in a pocket chart. Have index cards on hand to create word cards to substitute in the last line of the song. Ready, set, sing!

*(sung to the tune of "The Wheels on the Bus")*

The first sound of *duck* is /d/, /d/, /d/,
/d/, /d/, /d/,
/d/, /d/, /d/.
The first sound of *duck* is /d/, /d/, /d/
Just like [*doctor*].

## Under, Over, and On
### Understanding positional words

Use a duck's ability to dive under the water, paddle on the water, and fly over the water to practice positional words with youngsters. In advance, purchase or borrow a toy duck. Make a copy of the position cards on page 15, color them, and then cut them out. Put the pictures in a bag.

Have a child draw a picture card from the bag and tell the group the positional word on it. Then give her the duck and have her use it to demonstrate the position shown on her card. For example, if she chooses the card showing the word *under,* she may position the duck under a table, under a chair, or under a book. Continue in this manner until each child has had a turn. Then place the materials in the math center so students can do the activity again on their own.

## Floating Ducks
### Sorting

These fine-feathered friends provide fine-motor fun in addition to lots of sorting opportunities. To prepare, cut a supply of duck shapes in three different sizes from three colors of craft foam. Use a permanent marker to program each duck with one of these shapes: triangle, square, or circle. Cut out three lily pads from craft foam to use as sorting mats. Float the ducks in your water table. When a child visits the center, give him a pair of tongs. Instruct him to use the tongs to pick up the ducks and sort them onto the lily pad mats. Challenge students to sort the ducks by color, size, or shape attributes. It's a feathered frenzy!

# Crafty Quackers
*Following directions, using fine-motor skills*

These crafty quackers can be used as nametags, tabletop decor, or math manipulatives. Gather the materials listed below and then guide each child in assembling a cute waddling duck!

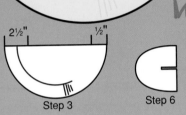

**Materials:**
9" paper plate
3" yellow craft foam circle (head)
1½" x 2" orange craft foam rectangle (bill)
3 yellow craft feathers

yellow tempera paint
paintbrush
permanent marker
scissors
stapler

**Steps:**
1. Paint a paper plate yellow. Allow the paint to dry.
2. Fold the paper plate in half.
3. Cut a 2½-inch slit in one end of the fold and a ½" slit at the other end as shown.
4. Use a permanent marker to draw an eye on each side of the head.
5. Insert the head into the longer slit; then staple it to the plate. Staple the feathers in the shorter slit to make tail feathers.
6. Trim the ends of the bill as you cut a small slit out of one end as shown.
7. Slide the duck's bill onto the head. Fold the bill down and staple it as shown.

2½"    ½"

Step 3        Step 6

# No Umbrella Needed
*Observing*

Do ducks carry umbrellas when it rains? No way! This observation helps little ones learn about a duck's special adaptation to wet weather and swimming. To begin, take youngsters outdoors and open an umbrella. Pour a cup of water over the umbrella and then talk about why people use umbrellas. Explain that ducks have a built-in umbrella, a special oil that their bodies make to cover their top feathers and make them waterproof. While still outside, wipe cooking oil on a craft feather. Use a dropper to drip water droplets on the feather. Encourage your students to watch as the droplets roll off the feather. Place several oiled feathers, eyedroppers, and a container of water on a table outside during recess. Encourage little ones to repeat the exploration using the supplies. What lucky ducks!

# A Dinner Fit for Ducks
*Counting to four*

Finish up your fun and feathery study with a ducky dinner. Place bowls of Gummy Worm candies, mini M&M's candies (bugs), fish-shaped crackers, and Cheerios cereal (frog eggs) on a table. Put a spoon in each bowl to use when serving. Label four cards each with a different numeral from 1 to 4. Place one card in front of each bowl as shown. Give each child a small cup and encourage her to waddle down the snack line, putting the corresponding number of edibles in her cup. After checking students' counting skills, let the flock feast!

## Position Cards
Use with "Under, Over, and On" on page 13.

under     over     on

# Gone Fishin'

This fishing-themed collection of ideas is sure to make a splash with your little ones!

*ideas contributed by Elizabeth Cook, St. Louis, MO*

## That's a Keeper!
### *Comparing lengths*

How will youngsters know which fish are keepers during this small-group activity? Why, by using a handy fish chart, of course! Laminate construction paper fish in three different sizes (pattern on page 20); then hot-glue a jumbo paper clip to each fish. Make a chart, similar to the one shown, that compares the lengths of the fish. Next, use a dowel rod and string to fashion a simple fishing pole; then tie a magnet to the end of the string. Spread the fish on the floor (the lake) and place the pole and chart nearby along with a cooler. Gather a small group of children. Have a child use the pole to catch a fish; then encourage her to place the fish on the chart to determine whether it is too small, too big, or just right. If the fish is just right, prompt her to place it in the cooler. If it is too big or too small, encourage her to toss it back in the lake.

Too Small

Just Right

Too Big

## Wonderful Worms
### *Developing letter-formation skills*

Worms are not only excellent bait for fishing, but they're also fantastic for practicing letter formation! Write different letters on each of several tagboard cards. Then laminate the cards for durability. Place in a container a variety of plastic worms or lengths of extra thick brown yarn. (For plastic worms, go to the fishing section of your local sports store.) Then place the worms and cards in a center. After a child chooses a card and identifies the letter, she places worms on the letter.

# Cracker Catch

### Identifying colors

This easy-to-prepare snack is sure to be popular! Give each youngster a paper plate containing a dollop of spreadable cheese and several pretzel sticks (fishing poles). Then give him a small disposable cup partially filled with colored fish-shaped crackers. The child dips a fishing rod into the spreadable cheese and then dips the cheese-covered end into the cup. He carefully removes the rod from the cup and identifies the color of the fish he's caught. Then he eats the fish and the pole as well! The youngster continues in the same way with the remaining rods and fish.

Janelle Daskal
Deer Park Teaching and Learning Center
Deerfield, IL

How I wish for a fish on my dish!

# Fish on a Dish

### Participating in a game

To play this game, gather a plastic dish and a fish cutout (pattern on page 20). If desired, also obtain a child's life jacket. Choose a volunteer to pretend to be a fisherman and invite him to put on the life jacket and hold the dish. Have the fisherman close his eyes and say the provided wish. While his eyes are closed, invite a child to place the fish cutout on the dish. Next, encourage the fisherman to open his eyes and try to guess, with help as needed, who placed the fish on his dish. When the correct child is chosen, repeat the game with two new youngsters.

# Bobbing Along

### Investigating items that float

Fishing bobbers are a nifty addition to your water table! Obtain bobbers in a variety of sizes and place them in your water table. Also place a variety of plastic or rubber fish in your table and set plastic cups and strainers nearby. A youngster visits the area and uses the various tools to explore the items.

# Tackle Box Math

### Identifying numbers, counting

Youngsters fill this tackle box with oodles of worms! Obtain a small plastic tackle box and place a number card in each section. Place the tackle box at a center along with a supply of brown yarn pieces (worms). A child places the appropriate number of worms in each section of the box.

Caught by Andy

# Catch of the Day!

### Writing one's name

This truly unique art project makes a fun hallway display! To begin, make two fish cutouts (pattern on page 20) for each child. Have each child decorate the cutouts; then staple the cutouts together, leaving a small opening. After the child stuffs the fish with paper shreds, staple the opening shut. Have each child glue his fish to a brown tagboard oval labeled "Caught by." Then encourage the child to add his name. Display the projects with the title "Catch of the Day!"

# Buying Bait

### Participating in dramatic play

This bait and tackle shop is open for business! Cut thick brown yarn into small sections; then place the resulting worms in a container. Cut out several blue construction paper copies of the minnow cards on the bottom of page 19. Place the minnows in a pail. Place the container and pail at a table decorated to resemble a bait and tackle shop. Also provide access to paper and pencils for writing orders, small plastic containers to hold individual purchases of worms and minnows, and money cutouts for purchases. If desired, provide other tackle and bait shop accessories, such as those shown. Youngsters visit the center and use the items to engage in dramatic play.

BAIT & TACKLE SHOP

Worms: 5¢ each
Minnows: 10¢ each

# Fabulous Fishing Hats

**Developing fine-motor skills**

Youngsters are sure to be proud of these finely decorated fishing hats! Have each child cut out an enlarged construction paper copy of the fishing hat pattern on page 21. Then provide access to glue; small, colorful craft feathers; and pom-poms. Encourage each child to glue the craft feathers and pom-poms to the hat, as shown, so they resemble fishing lures. When the glue is dry, display the projects on a bulletin board titled "Hats Off to Fishing!"

## Minnow Cards
Use with "Buying Bait" on page 18.

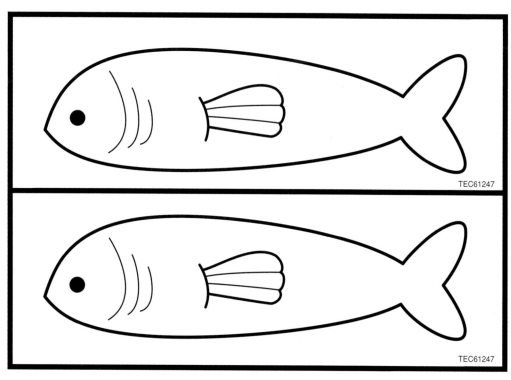

TEC61247

TEC61247

# Fish Pattern

Use with "That's a Keeper!" on page 16, "Fish on a Dish" on page 17, and "Catch of the Day!" on page 18.

TEC61247

20

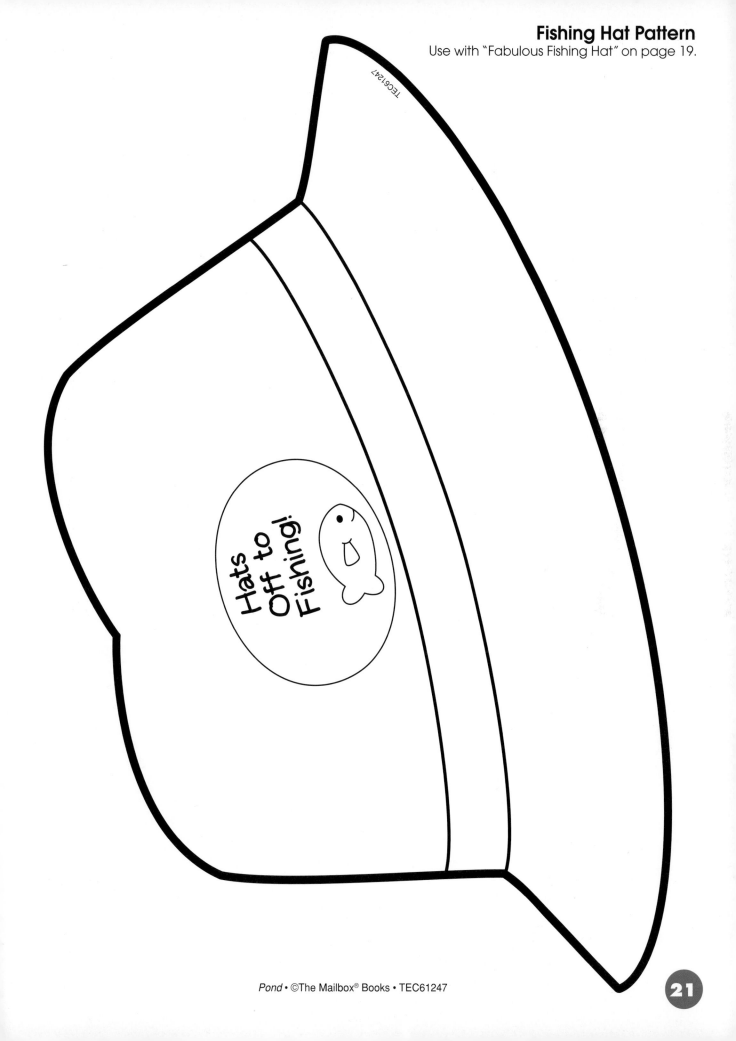

# Storytime

## Have You Seen My Duckling?

Written and Illustrated by Nancy Tafuri

*When a playful duckling swims away from its family, Mother Duck and her remaining ducklings scour the pond, questioning its inhabitants. Where is the missing duckling? It's cleverly nestled in the background in every scene!*

*ideas contributed by Roxanne LaBell Dearman*
*Western NC Early Intervention Program for Children*
*Who Are Deaf or Hard of Hearing*
*Charlotte, NC*

### Before You Read

Before sharing the story, cut out a yellow construction paper copy of the duckling pattern on page 25. Then attach the duckling to a wall or display in your classroom. Ask students if they've seen your duckling, encouraging them to scan the classroom for the lost critter. React with great excitement and joy when youngsters share the duckling's location. Next, explain that the storytime selection is about a duck that's also looking for a lost duckling. Finally, have little ones settle in for a read-aloud of the story.

There's your duckling!

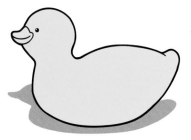

### After You Read

Cut a pond shape from blue bulletin board paper and place it in your circle-time area. Have each child color and cut out a personalized duckling pattern (see the pattern on page 25). Next, place all the ducklings on the pond. Gather youngsters around the pond and ask, "Have you seen [child's name]'s duckling?" Then invite the student to find her duckling. Continue in the same manner until each youngster has found her duckling.

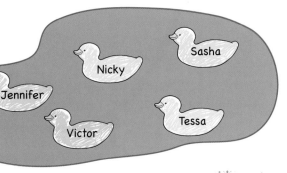

# One Duck Stuck

by Phyllis Root

*Oh, no! A duck is stuck in the muck—yuck! Watch as a host of animals who live near the marsh comes to help the duck get unstuck—what luck! Filled with engaging language and silly sounds, this counting book is sure to please preschoolers!*

## Before You Read

Splish, pleep, zing! The sounds made by the animals in this tale are quite unusual! For a fun introduction to the story, flip to the back of the book and find the two-page spread that shows nine different animals and the sounds they make. Without showing youngsters the illustrations, read aloud each sound and invite students to name animals that might make the sound. Without a doubt, your little ones' curiosity about the book is sure to grow!

Ada Goren
Winston-Salem, NC

## After You Read

**Following directions, participating in a story**

Here's a story follow-up that's just ducky! Have each student make a puppet that resembles the main character and use it during additional readings of the story! To make the puppet, have a child use a black crayon to draw two eyes and two eyebrows on a small white paper plate. Next, give him two beak shapes cut from orange construction paper. Help him stack the cutouts and glue them together at the top. Then help him glue the bottom beak on his paper plate. As a final touch, have him glue a white craft feather to the top back of the plate. Then tape a craft stick or plastic drinking straw to the back of the plate to serve as a handle. During each subsequent reading of the book, suggest that students raise their puppets as they chant the refrain, "Help! Help! Who can help?"

Ada Goren

# Once Upon A Story...

## In the Small, Small Pond

Introduce the topic of pond life to your youngsters with a frog's-eye peek at life in a small pond. Share *In the Small, Small Pond* by Denise Fleming. After a first read-through, ask students to name animals that use the pond as their home. Encourage students to name animals from the story as well as any others they might know. Record their responses on a sheet of chart paper. Next, reread the story outside where students will have plenty of room to move. As you read, stop after each animal's action and invite your students to act out the movements of the pond creatures. Your youngsters will be swimming like fish, hopping and diving like frogs, crawling and climbing like insects, and slithering like snakes!

## It's Mine!

Three frogs learn the value of sharing in Leo Lionni's *It's Mine!* After reading the book, help each child make this fun frog craft. For each frog, cut four green legs, one pink tongue, one white lily pad, and one blue pond from construction paper. Pinch one end of an empty toilet paper tube to bring opposite sides together; then staple it shut. Paint the tube green. When the paint is dry, use tacky glue to attach the four legs and the tongue as shown. Make eyes for the frog by gluing on two green pom-poms and two paper eyes as shown. Glue the frog to the lily pad cutout; then glue the lily pad to the pond. For a final touch, stamp a bug stamp or add a bug sticker to the end of the frog's tongue. Ribbit!

Trudy Buckalew—Three-Year-Olds
Bensalem Christian Day School
Bensalem, PA

TEC61247

TEC61247

TEC61247

 # More Pond

## Five Little Ducks

### Using props

A few fun props will get your preschoolers waddling on over to your listening area! Provide a tape of the traditional song "Five Little Ducks." Purchase some rubber duckies—five small ones and one larger one to be the mama. Add a large blue plastic bowl to the area too. Then invite a child to listen to and act out the song using the toy ducks and the blue bowl pond.

Cathy Consford—Director
Buda Primary Early Learning Center
Buda, TX

## Adorable Ducks

### Matching

Use a permanent marker to program the bottom of each of several plastic ducks with a different symbol of your choice. Then program an equal number of plastic lids with matching symbols. Place the ducks in your water table and the lids nearby. A youngster chooses a duck and sets it on the corresponding lid. She continues until all the ducks are resting on their matching lids.

Jill Beattie
Apple Place Nursery School
Chambersburg, PA

# Ideas

## Hop to It!
### *Symbol recognition*

Invite your youngsters to join in some frog follies with a gross-motor activity that also reinforces basic skills. In advance, cut out several large construction paper lily pads. Program each lily pad with a different shape, number, or letter. If desired, laminate the pads for durability. Lay the pads on the floor of your circle-time area and then secure each pad to the floor with clear Con-Tact paper. Have your little froggies stand in a circle around the lily pads. Call a child's name and a symbol programmed on one of the lily pads. Then have that child hop like a frog to the appropriate pad, name the symbol, and then hop back to the group. Ribbit!

Deborah Garmon
Groton, CT

## Lily Pad Listening
### *Following oral directions*

No doubt your preschoolers will jump at the chance to play the part of a frog! Give each child a lily pad shape cut from green poster board or craft foam. Direct your little frogs to jump on or off their lily pads. Ask them to hold their lily pads in front of, behind, or beside them. Or direct your junior frogs to put their lily pads on their heads, knees, or backs. To increase the challenge, give two-step directions such as "Put one knee on your lily pad and one knee on the floor." When your little frogs are tired, have them sit on their lily pads and rest. Ribbit!

Kelly Thompson—Three- and Four-Year-Olds
Head Start
Fort Dodge, IA

# Frog Fun!

### Using props

These frogs on a log are sure to liven up the favorite tune "Five Speckled Frogs." Your youngsters may even want to make their own song props! To make a prop, use a brown crayon to color a paper towel tube to resemble a log. Use a utility knife to cut five slits in the tube, each the width of a craft stick. Glue the log onto a piece of blue construction paper cut into a pond shape. On the pond, glue a copy of the song. To make the frog puppets, attach a frog sticker to each of five craft sticks; then insert the craft sticks into the log. When singing the song, take out a frog from the log with each consecutive verse and have it jump into the pond. Splash!

Ann Bovenkamp—Preschool
Young Ideas Preschool
Newton, IA

# Turtle Togs

### Investigating living things

These turtle costumes are sure to tantalize tots! To make one, cut a two-foot circle from heavy paper or poster board. Have a child use geometric-shaped objects, such as various blocks, to print patterns on the circle to resemble a turtle's shell. Next, cut a brown paper grocery bag into a simple vest. Staple the shell onto the back of the open vest. Transform a tot into a turtle by helping him slip on the vest; then encourage him to commence to "crawling" or "swimming." Whether you make one or many costumes, your youngsters will enjoy some "turtle-rific" dramatic play outdoors.

Julie A. Koczur, Norman, OK

## Five Little Ducks: An Old Rhyme
### Illustrated by Pamela Paparone

*While Mother Duck is busy doing chores, one by one her five little ducks are disappearing! Young readers will join in this tune's repetitive text and rejoice with Mother Duck when the little ones return.*

Rub-a-dub-dub—there's a duck in the tub! This idea provides hands-on counting practice and also offers a home-school connection. In advance, use the duck pattern on page 40 to make several tagboard tracers. After sharing the book, have each child trace a duck pattern on a piece of craft foam (or a sponge) and then cut it out. Invite groups of five children at a time to take their ducks to your water table. Encourage them to sing the song and act out the story with their ducks. Afterward encourage each child to take his duck home to remind him to share the song with his family—and to have as a bathtub buddy!

## From Tadpole to Frog

Sing this simple song at circle time to help youngsters learn the life cycle of a frog. Sing the song and show sequencing cards that depict the transformation. (For a set of cards, see page 41.) Now hop to it!

*(sung to the tune of "Twinkle, Twinkle, Little Star")*

The tadpole hatches from an egg.
Then it sprouts two strong back legs.
Soon it gets its front legs too.
Can you guess? What do they do?
Now the tadpole is a frog
Jumping on a great big log!

adapted from a song by
Julie Hughes—Three-Year-Olds
Baxter YMCA Preschool
Indianapolis, IN

29

## Let's Hear It for Frogs!

Sing this lively springtime song and invite youngsters to perform the froggy actions as directed.

*(sung to the tune of "Do You Know the Muffin Man?")*

Oh, look! I see some [hopping] frogs,
Some [hopping] frogs, some [hopping] frogs!
Oh, look! I see some [hopping] frogs
[Hopping] around the pond!

Sing additional verses, replacing the underlined word with other action words, such as *dancing, croaking,* and *sleeping.*

## I'm a Little Froggy

Hop to it and teach your youngsters this little ditty! Ribbit!

*(sung to the tune of "I'm a Little Teapot")*

I'm a little froggy,
Slick and green.
I once was a tadpole,
As you have seen.
Then I grew some strong legs
While swimming about,
And now I'm a frog.
Hurray, let's shout!
"Ribbit!"

Cathie Rubley Hart—Gr. K
Westwood Hills Elementary
Waynesboro, VA

# Dinner for Duck

This little song is simply ducky! Before leading youngsters in singing the song, explain that some ducks feed by tipping upside down so that their heads are underwater and they can reach tasty water plants and insects.

*(sung to the tune of "How Much Is That Doggie in the Window?")*

Oh, look at that ducky in the water.
It makes a fun quack, quack, quack sound.
It flaps and then dives to look for dinner.
Its tail is up; its head is down!

adapted from an idea by Lori Henson
Education Corner
Wichita, KS

# Just Ducky!
### Art

Caution: Little ones could go "quackers" over this adorable duck project! To make the duck, copy the pattern from page 42 onto white construction paper. Color the bill orange and then use yellow tempera paint to sponge-paint the duck. (For a duck with texture, sponge-paint with a mixture of one part yellow tempera paint, two parts glue, and two parts nonmentholated shaving cream.) When the paint is dry, cut out the duck and tape a craft stick to the back of the cutout for support.

To make the water, fold in half a thin white paper plate. Scallop the fold line without cutting into the plate rim. Then unfold the plate, press it flat, and sponge-paint it with blue tempera paint. When the paint is dry, refold the plate, slip the duck into the water, and display the project on a tabletop. Quack, quack!

31

# Ribbit!

### *Art*

Here's a spring craft worth croaking about—especially if your class is doing a frog unit or learning about the color green. Begin by using a green crayon to color both sides of a small paper plate; then fold the plate in half. Next, use a marker to color a wooden ice cream spoon red. Cut out white paper eyes and green paper legs. Color a black circle on each white circle; then glue the eyes and legs to the plate as shown. For extra fun glue a plastic fly onto the spoon before taping it to the plate. Display the frogs on a blue background, or use them to hop into language fun with your favorite frog fingerplays and songs.

Debi Luke—Four-Year-Olds
Fairmount Nursery School
Syracuse, NY

# Lily Pad Look-Alikes

### *Art*

Leapin' lily pads! These froggy hangouts look like the real thing! To make one, cut a triangle shape from the rim of a small, thick paper plate. Then paint the plate green. Next, use food coloring to tint a container of water red. Fold a coffee filter in half several times, dip one corner of the folded filter into the water, and then unfold the filter. When the painted plate and filter are dry, gather and twist the center of the filter and tape (or staple) it near the point where the triangle was cut out. Hey, come on over to my pad!

Nancy M. Lotzer
Farmers Branch, TX

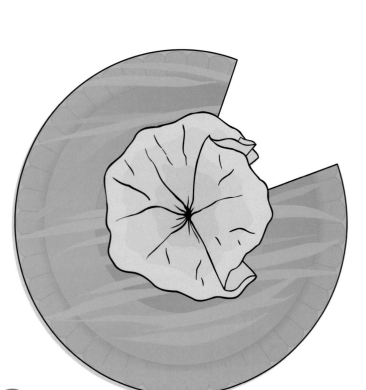

## Turtle Love
### *Art*
Youngsters are sure to love making as many of these terrific turtles as their hearts desire! To make one, simply make a fist and then dip your knuckles and thumb into a shallow pan of green or brown paint. Press your knuckles and thumb onto paper. When the paint is dry, use markers or more paint to add facial features, legs, and details to the turtle's shell. Youngsters can make all types of turtles with this easy project!

Al Trautman—ECEEN (K3–K5)
Milwaukee, WI

## Turtle Time
### *Art*
These turtles will suit your little ones to a T. Sponge-paint a paper-plate half the colors of your choice. From green construction paper, cut a turtle head, a tail, and two legs. Glue the paper pieces to the back of the painted plate. Add a paper eye to the turtle's head to complete the project. Top off your turtle time by reading aloud any of the tales about Franklin the turtle by Paulette Bourgeois.

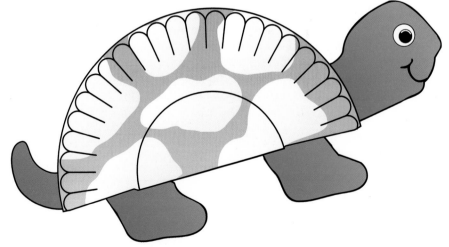

# We're Talkin' Turtles!
## *Art*

Don't be a slowpoke to try out this turtle craft! To get started, collect soft cardboard produce separators found in boxes of apples at your local grocer. Cut the cardboard apart so that you have a class supply of shapes to serve as turtle shells. To make one turtle, use tempera paint to paint a shell green or brown. From construction paper, cut out four turtle legs, a head, and a tail; then glue the shapes to the underside of the dry shell. Use markers and paper eyes to add details to the legs and head. Display the projects on a bulletin board paper pond along with rocks and a collection of Franklin books by Paulette Bourgeois.

Barbara Meyers
Fort Worth Country Day
Fort Worth, TX

# Dazzling Dragonflies
## *Art*

Dazzle 'em with these easy-to-make dragonflies! To make one, use markers to add eyes and some color to an old-fashioned wooden clothespin. Next, tie a ten-inch length of monofilament line into a loop. Also cut two rectangles (about 5" x 8") from different colors of cellophane. Holding the clothespin with the open end up, slide the loop and then the two cellophane pieces into the clothespin. Dangle these dainty insects in front of a sunny window.

Sharon M. Coulter
Park Place Children's Center
Muncie, IN

# In the Pond

Here's the next best thing to having a classroom pond! Drape a table with a blue paper tablecloth. Tape student-made lily pads (page 32) and peekaboo frogs to the top of the pond. Below the pond's surface, display greenery, bubble wrap frog eggs (page 4), and student-decorated fish and frog cutouts. Ribbit!

Nancy M. Lotzer, Farmers Branch, TX

Get your ducks in a row with this attendance display. Mount student-fingerpainted paper onto a background to resemble a pond; then add details, such as twisted brown paper (logs) and fringed green-paper (grass). To make her duck, a child sponge-paints half a paper plate tan. Next, she cuts out a head and beak from construction paper and then glues the pieces onto the dried plate. Personalize each duck and then store it in a tub near the display. As each student arrives in the morning, she takes her duck from the tub; then her parent pins it to the pond. You'll be able to tell at a glance which ducklings are at school!

To make this easy-to-adapt display, have each student color a personalized paper plate green and then glue an illustrated frog head, two front legs, and two back legs to it (patterns on page 43). Then instruct her to write an assigned letter on a lily pad and add illustrations of words that begin with that letter. Display students' work as shown.

Megan Carney, Multiple Intelligences School, Worcester, MA

Spark students' creativity with this pond project! Instruct students to sponge-paint a white-backed board green and blue. Then have them paint grassy plants and post paper rocks and logs. Over the next several days, invite youngsters to add desired details to the scene. For example, they might make construction paper cattails and paper plate turtles. They might also glue triangles to old CDs so that the CDs resemble fish and cover packing peanuts with foil to make minnows. The possibilities are endless!

Ruth Rigenhagen, Quality Schools International, Kosice, Slovakia

# KIDS IN THE KITCHEN

Put on your apron and step into the kitchen—with your kids, of course! What's on the menu? A generous portion of learning opportunities served up with a batch of fun. Savor the following hands-on cooking activities, perfectly measured for preschool fun and teacher ease.

## Here's what to do:

- Collect the necessary ingredients and utensils using the lists on one of the recipe cards below.
- Follow the teacher preparation guidelines for that cooking activity.
- Photocopy the step-by-step recipe cards on page 38 or 39.
- Color the cards; then cut them out.
- Display the cards on a bulletin board or chart in your cooking area so that the students can see the directions for the recipe you've selected.
- Discuss the directions with a small group of kids; then encourage them to get cooking!

## Learning has never been so delicious!

### Delicious Lily Pad

**Ingredients for one:**
slice-and-bake sugar cookie dough
green-tinted icing
flower-shaped cake decoration

**Utensils and supplies:**
paper plate for each child
jumbo craft stick for each child
knife *(for teacher use only)*
oven *(for teacher use only)*

**Teacher preparation:**
Slice sugar cookie dough; then cut out a small triangle shape from each slice to create a lily pad. Bake the cookies as directed on the package. Arrange the ingredients and utensils near the step-by-step recipe cards (page 38).

Lari Junkin—Three-Year-Olds, Cathedral School
Natchez, MS

### Froggy Face

**Ingredients for one:**
English muffin half
green-tinted cream cheese
2 thin banana slices
4 mini chocolate chips
1"-wide strip of a red Fruit Roll-Ups fruit snack
3 chocolate cereal puffs
diluted lemon juice (optional)

**Utensils and supplies:**
paper plate for each child
plastic knife
bowl
spoon

**Teacher preparation:**
Use green food coloring to tint a container of cream cheese green. Cut the fruit snacks into one-inch-wide strips. Lastly, slice the bananas into the bowl. If desired, toss the banana slices with diluted lemon juice to prevent browning. Then arrange the ingredients, paper plates, and plastic knife near the step-by-step recipe cards (page 39).

Melissa Guthrie—Preschool, Trinity Lutheran School, Newport News, VA

# Recipe Cards

Use with "Delicious Lily Pad" on page 37.

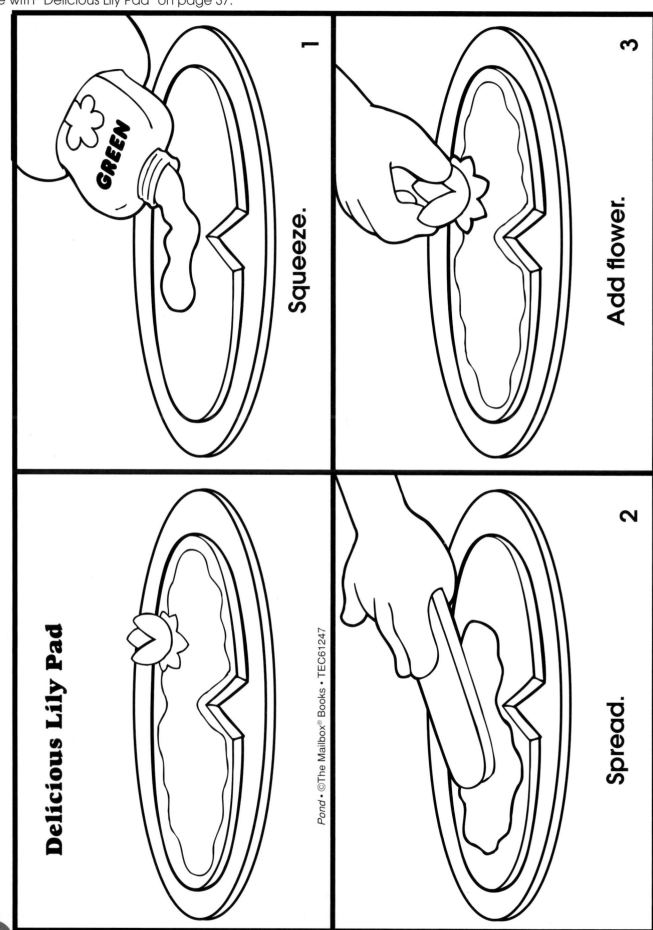

1 Squeeze.

2 Spread.

3 Add flower.

Delicious Lily Pad

*Pond* • ©The Mailbox® Books • TEC61247

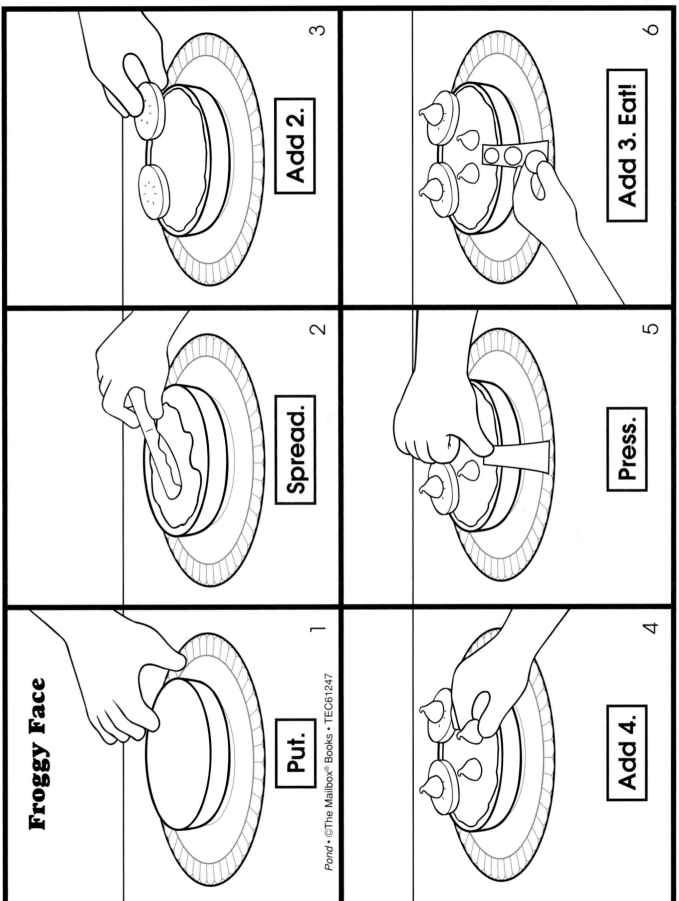

**Froggy Face**

3 | Add 2.

2 | Spread.

1 | Put.

6 | Add 3. Eat!

5 | Press.

4 | Add 4.

*Pond* • ©The Mailbox® Books • TEC61247

# Duck Pattern
Use with "*Five Little Ducks: An Old Rhyme*" on page 29.

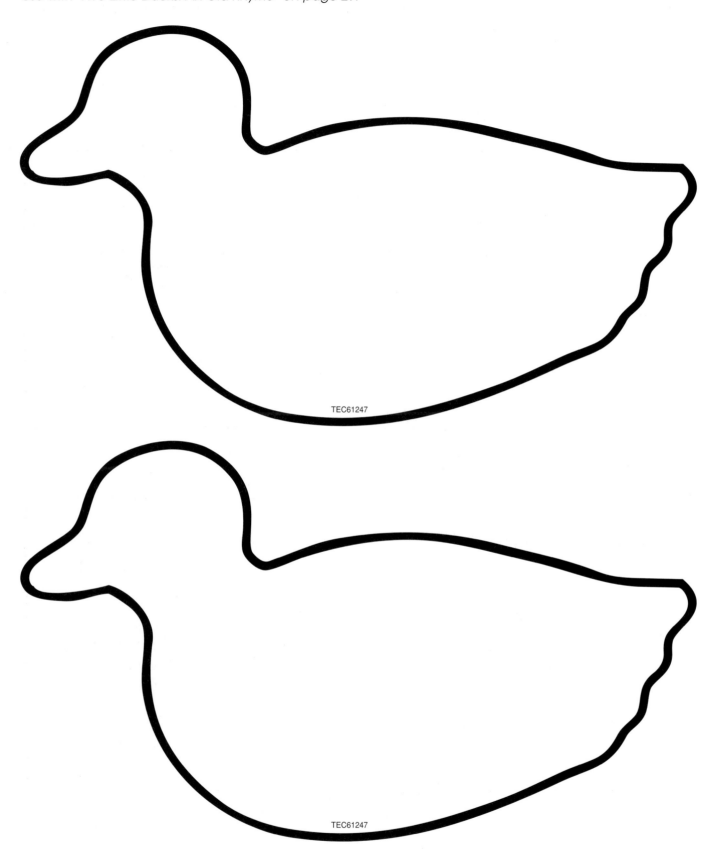

TEC61247

TEC61247

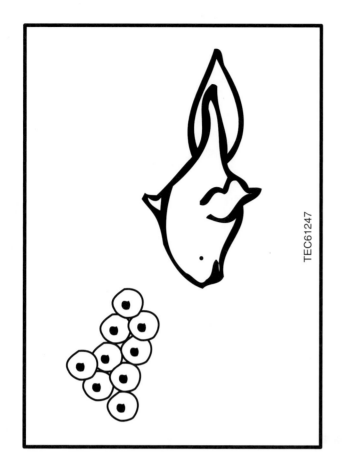

TEC61247

TEC61247

TEC61247

TEC61247

# Duck Pattern

Use with "Just Ducky!" on page 31.

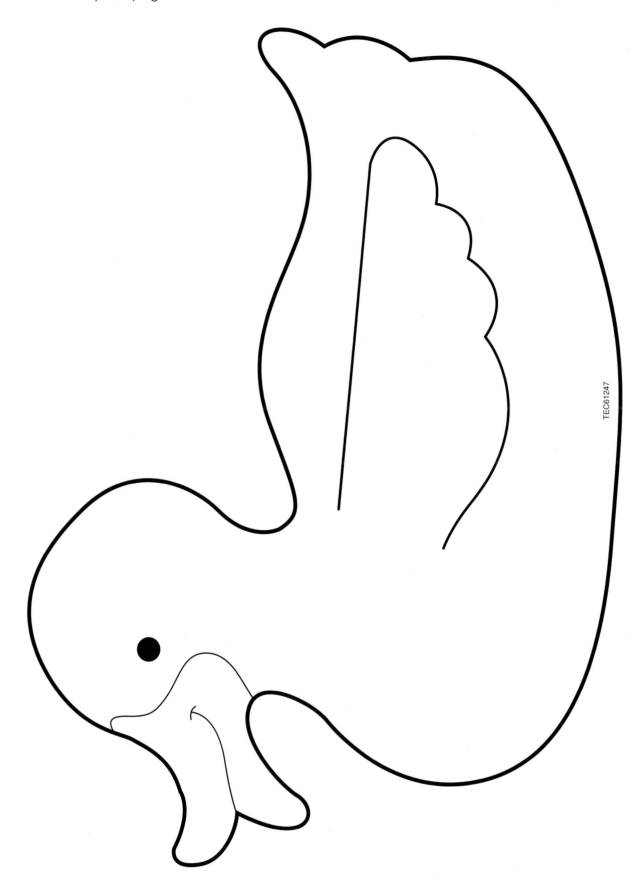

TEC61247

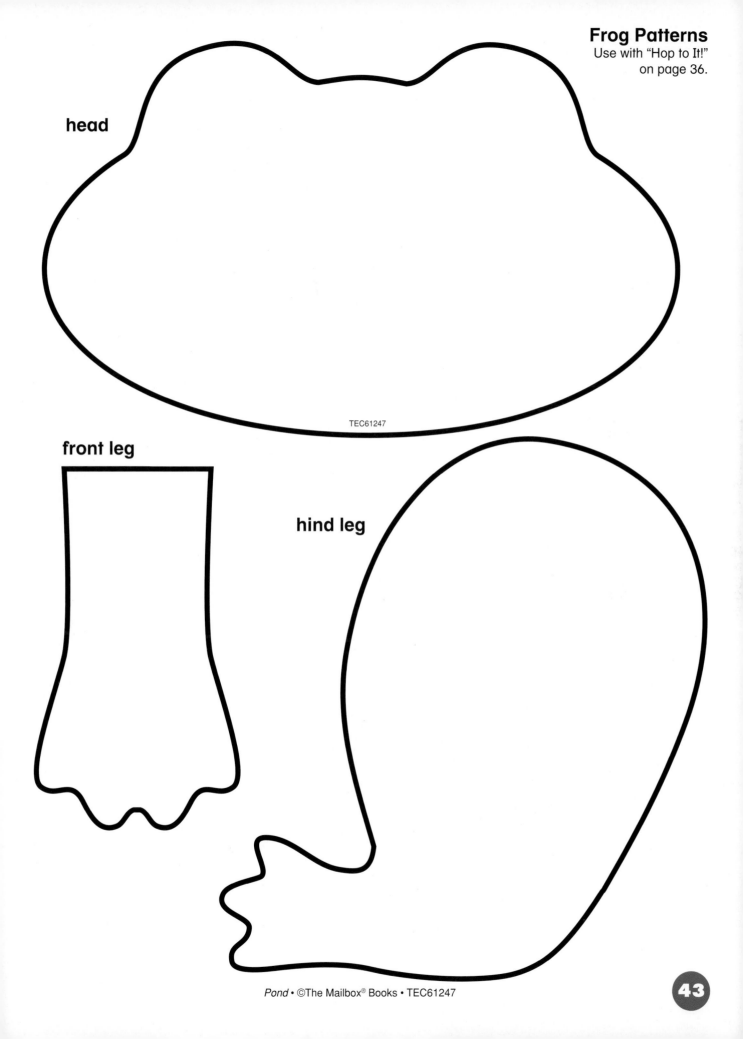

**Frog Patterns**
Use with "Hop to It!"
on page 36.

head

front leg

hind leg

TEC61247

# Duck Booklet

## Materials Needed for Each Student

copy of pages 45–46
crayons
scissors
access to a stapler

## How to Use Pages 45 and 46

Focus on the illustrations of the duck life cycle in *Make Way for Ducklings* by Robert McCloskey as youngsters create this fun shaped booklet. Give each child a copy of pages 45 and 46. Read the text aloud and help each student follow the directions below to make a booklet.

## Directions for Each Booklet

1. Help each student color and cut out the booklet backing, cover, and pages.
2. Sequence the booklet pages and cover and then staple them to the booklet backing.
3. Read the booklet with the class.

## Finished Sample

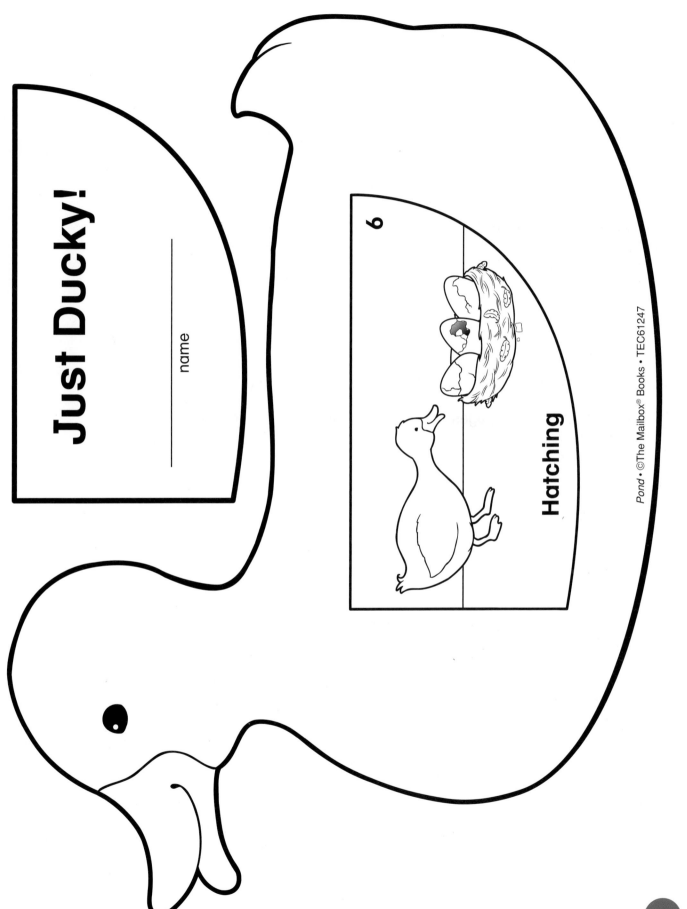

# Just Ducky!

name

6

Hatching

*Pond* • ©The Mailbox® Books • TEC61247

**Booklet pages**

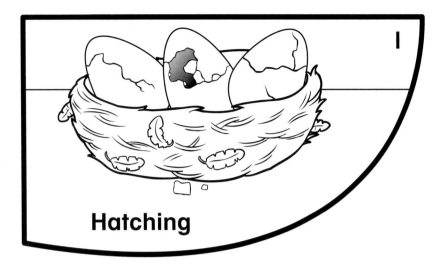

1

Hatching

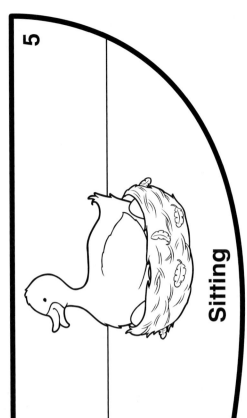

5

Sitting

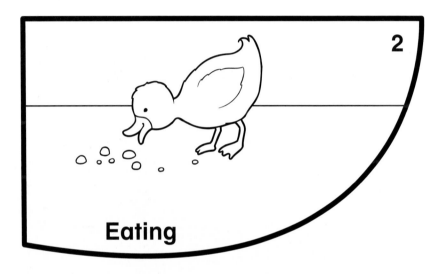

2

Eating

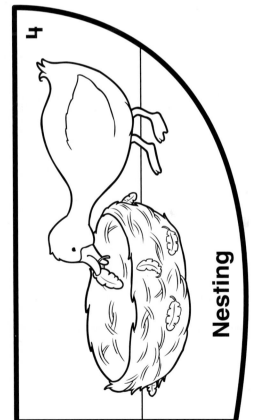

4

Nesting

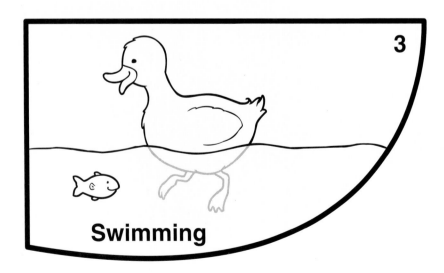

3

Swimming

Name _____

# Down by the Pond

Count.

Color the graph to show how many.

Name_____

# Pond Scene

Color the pictures that rhyme in each row.

Pond • ©The Mailbox® Books • TEC61247